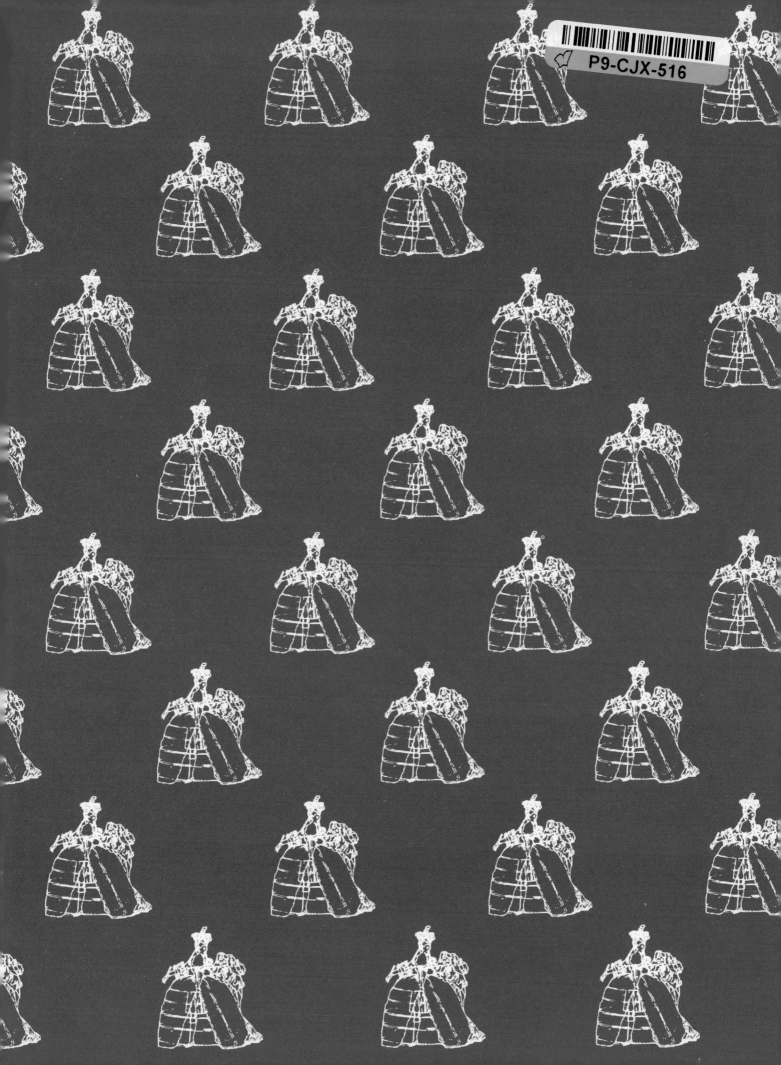

CLOTHES

FOR WORK, PLAY & DISPLAY

Series Editor:
David Salariya was born in Dundee, Scotland, where he studied illustration and printmaking, concentrating on book design in his postgraduate year. He later completed a further postgraduate course in art education at Sussex University in England. He has illustrated a wide range of books on botanical, historical, and mythical subjects. He has designed and created many new series of children's books for publishers in the U.K. and overseas. In 1989, he established his own publishing company, The Salariya Book Company Ltd. He lives in Brighton, England, with his wife, the illustrator Shirley Willis.

Author:
Jacqueline Morley is a graduate of Oxford University in England. She has taught English and History and now works as a free-lance translator and writer with a special interest in the history of everyday life. She has written historical fiction and nonfiction for children. She assisted in the installation of the costume display at Warwick County Museum in Warwick, England, and advised on the Fashion Gallery at Brighton Museum in Brighton, England.

Consultant:
Rosemary Harden is assistant keeper at the Museum of Costume in Bath, England. She has also worked in the Textiles and Dress Department at the Victoria and Albert Museum in London.

First published in 1992
by Franklin Watts

Franklin Watts
95 Madison Avenue
New York, NY 10016

Series Editor	David Salariya
Senior Editor	Ruth Taylor
Book Editor	Vicki Power
Consultant	Rosemary Harden
Artists	Vanda Baginska
	Mark Bergin
	John James
	Carolyn Scrace
	Gerald Wood

Artists
Vanda Baginska p 8-9; **Mark Bergin** p 12-13, p 24-25, p 32-33, p 40-41, p 42-43; **John James** p 14-15, p 16-17, p 20-21, p 26-27, p 38-39; **Carolyn Scrace** p 18-19, 22-23, p 34-35, p 36-37; **Gerald Wood** p 6-7, p 10-11, p 28-29, p 30-31.

Library of Congress Cataloging-in-Publication Data

Morley, Jacqueline.
    Clothes for work, play & display / by Jacqueline Morley.
        p.   cm. – (Timelines)
    Includes bibliographical references and index.
    Summary: Traces the development of clothing from prehistoric times to future possibilities, describing adaptatio brought about by social, political, and technological changes
    ISBN 0-531-15249-9. – ISBN 0-531-11170-9 (lib. bdg.)
    1. Costume – History – Juvenile literature. 2. Clothing dress – History – Juvenile literature. [1. Clothing and dress 2. Costume – History.] I. Title. II. Title: Clothes for work, play, and display. III. Series: Timelines (Franklin Watts, In
GT518.M67 1992   92-485
391 -- dc20   CIP

TIMELINES
CLOTHES

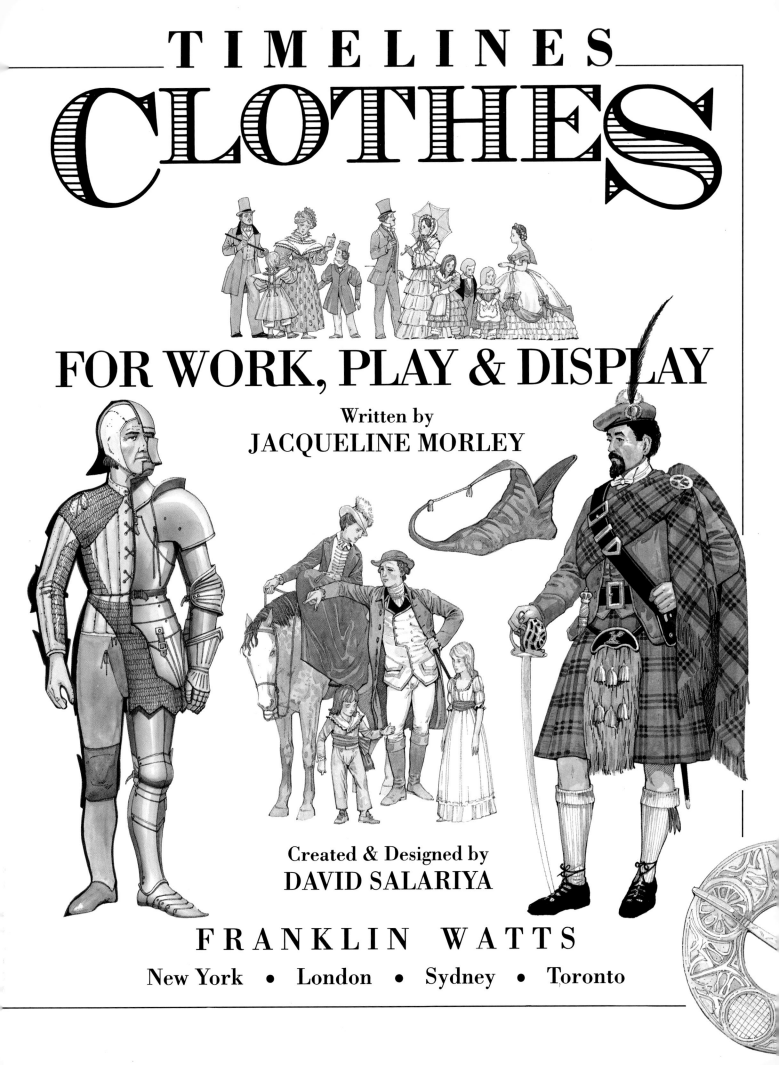

FOR WORK, PLAY & DISPLAY

Written by
JACQUELINE MORLEY

Created & Designed by
DAVID SALARIYA

FRANKLIN WATTS
New York • London • Sydney • Toronto

CONTENTS

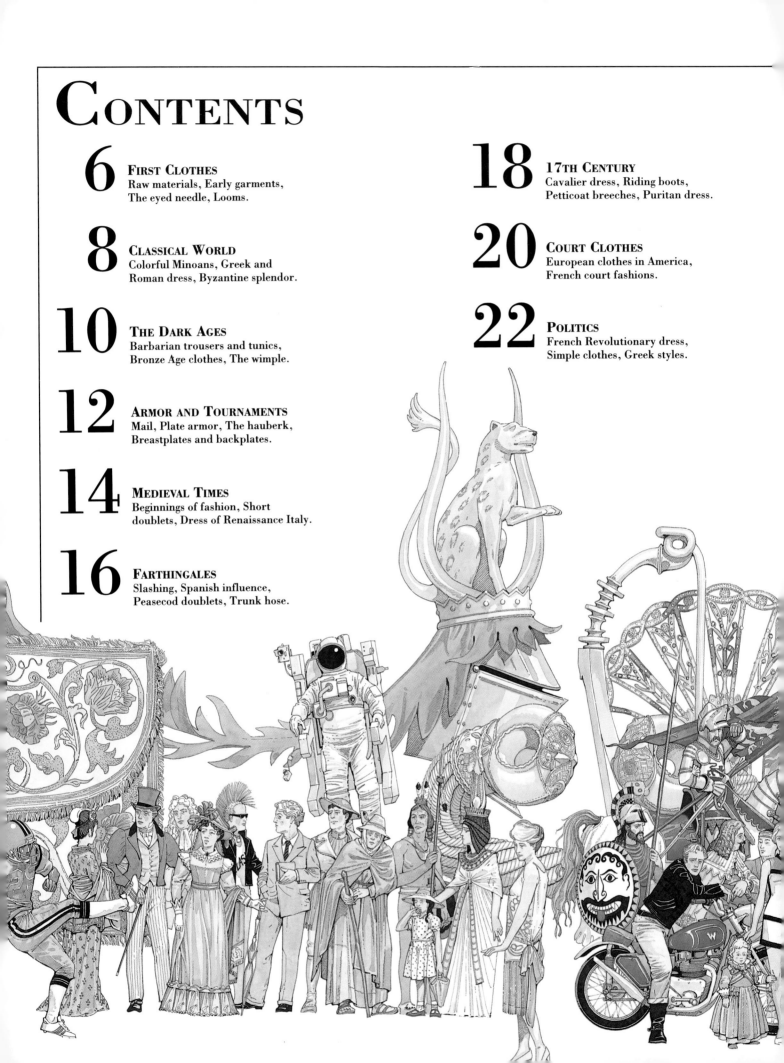

FIRST CLOTHES

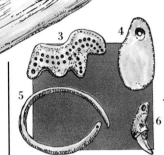

△ SCRAPING A SKIN to clean it before tanning.

WHY DO HUMAN BEINGS WEAR CLOTHES? To keep warm is the obvious answer, but there is more to the story of clothes than that. Evidence from Paleolithic sites of over 23,000 years ago shows that people decorated their garments of animal skins with shells and beads. Right from the start people tried to make their clothes attractive. An antler headdress has also survived, worn perhaps by a hunter, which suggests that wearing special dress for doing a job or performing a role is very old.

△ IVORY FIGURE, 8,000 to 10,000 years old, in a fur garment like an Eskimo's (*right*).

△ PALEOLITHIC ANTLER HEADDRESS. It may have been used in hunting, in battle, or for a ritual.

1 BONE TOOL for piercing skins before sewing.
2 Bone needle.
3 & 4 Bone pendants.
5 Ivory bracelet.
6 Animal-tooth bead.

The invention of bone needles was the first step toward fitted clothes. The next was the weaving of cloth. It seems likely that this began in early Neolithic times, when people first grew plants and kept flocks for wool.

△ PALEOLITHIC FAMILY wearing skins. The children's clothes are decorated with seashells and the man's clothes with ivory beads and fox teeth.

△ POUNDING BARK TO MAKE BARK CLOTH. Before weaving was known, materials such as bark were used to make clothes.

▽ NEOLITHIC NECKLACE made of shells.

Neolithic traders bartered cloth and body ornaments. They probably understood another of the uses of dress – to enable us to show that we have more style than the next person.

▽ HORIZONTAL LOOMS like this one were used in ancient Egypt for weaving fine linen.

◁ NEOLITHIC CLOTHES of skin and woven cloth, 6000 B.C.

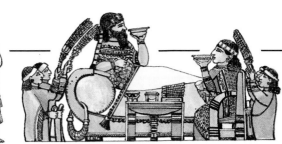

△ SUMERIAN NOBLE and soldier, about 2500 B.C. The tufted skirt may copy earlier garments made of skins.

△ THIS BABYLONIAN COUPLE (*left*) wear material draped around their bodies. Assyrian nobleman on the right.

△ ASSYRIAN KING AND QUEEN from the 7th century B.C., wearing diadems and patterned garments.

△ ASSYRIANS WORE SLEEVED TUNICS draped with shawls. Hair and beards were arranged in rows of curls.

△ A SILVER DISH showing a man in trousers, a garment from Asia brought to Mesopotamia.

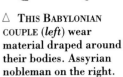

△ EGYPTIAN ROBES, of semitransparent linen, knotted at the waist.

The Sumerians and the ancient Egyptians are the first civilized peoples of whose clothes we know anything. The art of the Sumerians, and of the Babylonians and Assyrians whose empires followed theirs in Mesopotamia (modern Iraq), is mainly concerned with kings and their armies, so it is not possible to be sure how ordinary people dressed. With the ancient Egyptians we are luckier, because they painted everyday scenes on the walls of their tombs. Their way of life and style of dress varied little for over 3,000 years.

△ EGYPTIAN WOMAN in a robe of fine linen, c.1300 B.C. Her male attendants wear skirts with pleated aprons.

▽ PHARAOH TUTAN-KHAMEN AND HIS WIFE, about 1355 B.C. The use of magnificent dress to show a person's power and status is as old as the very earliest civilizations.

▽ WORKERS WORE ONLY A LOINCLOTH. Working women wore a simple sheath dress.

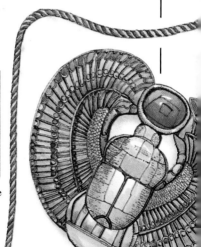

◁ RICH EGYPTIANS wore wigs, jewelry, and makeup, but only kings and queens wore such resplendent crowns.

SCARAB AND FALCON PENDANTS belonging to Tutankhamen.

EGYPTIANS regarded their kings as gods. Crowns and jewelry were the outward signs of this. The falcon was the emblem of the sun god. The beetle symbolized eternal life.

CLASSICAL WORLD

△ MINOAN WOMEN with flowing hair and bare breasts. Minoan priest-king (*below*).

THE MINOANS, who lived on the Mediterranean island of Crete, were a nation of sea traders whose history began almost as long ago as that of the Sumerians and Egyptians. They must have been a lively and original people. The paintings and clay figures excavated at their royal palace at Knossos (c.1500 B.C.) show that their close-fitting, brightly colored clothes were quite unlike those of Egypt or Babylon. The women wore laced bodices and flounced skirts. Both men and women squeezed their waists into very tight wide belts, which seem to have been the world's first corsets.

△ GREEK HUNTSMAN, 5th century B.C., in a short cloak called a chlamys and a traveller's hat.

△ GREEK WORKERS wore few clothes, or none if it was easier.

△ GREEK WOMEN wore their hair bound up. This girl of 470 B.C. has her hair in a bun.

△ DECKING THE BRIDE, from a 5th-century box. The child wears a Doric chiton, while the women wear Ionic chitons in soft, fine cloth.

1 The Ionic chiton.
2 The narrower Doric chiton.

▽ GREEK NECKLACE.

△ THE BRIDE WEARS her himation over her head, as women did outdoors.

△ THE GROOM is wearing a himation only.

▽ WEDDING GUESTS WEAR long cloaks called himations. The male torchbearer wears a long ceremonial chiton.

▽ A FIBULA, or brooch.

△ GREEK SOLDIER in a leather tunic worn over a short chiton, a helmet and shin guards.

The graceful clothes of the ancient Greeks were variations of a basic tunic, called a chiton. This was an oblong piece of material, fastened by brooches on one or both shoulders. It was usually gathered in at the waist by a girdle, and then bloused out. In early times chitons were woolen, but as the Greeks grew richer, many people wore fine linen. Cloaks were worn outdoors. Wealthy people wore sandals but went barefoot indoors.

The Etruscans, who flourished in Italy from the seventh century B.C., seem, from their fitted tunics and boots, to have come from Asia. Under Greek influence in the fifth century B.C., they began to wear more draped clothes.

◁ EARLY ETRUSCAN. Dress shows Cretan or Asiatic influence.

△ ETRUSCANS, 5TH CENTURY. The cloak became the Roman toga.

△ ROMAN SCHOOLBOY IN A DALMATIC, a tunic with wide sleeves worn from A.D. C.100.

△ MOSAIC SHOWING A ROMAN GYMNAST in clothes very like Greek and Roman underwear.

▽ MAN IN A TOGA, a large semicircular garment. The woman's tunic resembles an Ionic chiton.

The Romans, like the Greeks, wore draped clothes. The toga was a male garment, worn on its own in early times. It was the mark of a Roman citizen. A slave was not allowed to wear one. Wealthy Roman women wore embroidered tunics, sleeved, or pinned in the Greek style.

△ ROMAN STREET MUSICIANS. Working people wore loincloths or tunics, and cloaks.

▽ RICH FABRICS AND JEWELS FROM THE EAST made Byzantine dress luxurious.

In Imperial Rome (from 27 B.C.), many people could afford to dress richly. They wore cotton from India and silk from the East, decorated with gold and gems. When Rome fell to the barbarians in A.D. 476, a very stiff, heavily ornamented version of Roman dress survived in the eastern part of the empire, ruled from Byzantium.

△ ROMAN GOLD finger rings and earring.

▽ BYZANTINE RIDER, 4th century A.D.

△ BYZANTINE NOBLES. The contrasting square on the cloak at the right is a sign of rank.

▷ BYZANTINES WEARING TROUSERS. Romans hated trousers because barbarians wore them.

THE DARK AGES

NORTH OF THE ROMAN EMPIRE lived people whom the Romans regarded as barbarians. Bronze Age burials of 3,000 years ago, found in Denmark, tell us what these northerners were wearing at a time long before the Roman Empire was founded. There is then a gap in our knowledge until the time of the Celtic tribes that were known to the Greeks and Romans. Like the Germanic peoples who moved over Europe in the first to the fifth centuries A.D., the Celts wore tunics and loose trousers often bound to their legs with bands.

△ BRONZE AGE MAN wearing cloak, tunic, felted hat, and foot wrappings.

◁ DETAIL OF Celtic gold torque.

△ BRONZE AGE CLOTHES. The girl's skirt is made of woolen cords. The woman's jacket is embroidered at the neck and sleeves. The man has a high-crowned hat.

△ THE CELTS WERE WARLIKE and loved display in both war gear and ornaments such as armbands and torques.

Celtic warriors tattooed their skin and wore long hair.

Their clothes were often checkered and brightly colored.

The Germanic invaders soon copied the luxurious habits of the Roman Empire. The Franks in Gaul (modern France) and the Anglo-Saxons in Britain wore tunics derived from the Roman dalmatic. The sea-faring Vikings wore furs, tunics, and leggings.

◁ VIKING NECKLACE

◁ VIKING WOMAN. Over a linen petticoat she wears two rectangles of cloth.

▽ BYZANTINE TUNICS were copied by Germanic nobles during the Dark Ages.

△ THIS VIKING MERCHANT wears baggy trousers and a cloak.

△ BETWEEN A.D. 500 AND 1100, clothes altered little. Tunic lengths varied.

△ STYLES OF DRESS.
A Franks, 6th c.
B Anglo-Saxons, 9th c.
C Normans, 11th c.

By the twelfth century, tunics and overtunics were still worn by both men and women, but the clothes of rich people began to be more luxurious. Knights returning from the crusades brought news of the sumptuous clothes of the East. Trade was increasing. Silks and furs were available for the rich. Poor people wore rough, homespun cloth.

△ TWELFTH-CENTURY NOBLEWOMAN. False hair was used to make braids longer.

△ WOMAN in the sleeveless overgown and hair net worn late in the 13th century.

△ STAINED GLASS, 13th century, showing a man who has taken off his tunic and is working in his braies. Peasants still wore their braies baggy.

△ DOOR CARVING, c.1200, of a noble wearing a long mantle.

△ TWELFTH-CENTURY NOBLE. His shaped tunic is laced up behind. Sleeves often flared out into wide cuffs or into dangling ends, which were so long that they were tied in knots.

△ SHEPHERDS dressed in short tunics, baggy hose, and hooded capes of hard-wearing wool. These were the working clothes of ordinary people throughout the Middle Ages.

Twelfth-century nobles wore long tunics, the women's often trailing on the ground. Sleeves were very long. Garments were laced tight over the chest and bound with pleated belts. Thirteenth-century styles were less exaggerated. Men's tunics were shorter. Women's gowns were unbelted and fell loosely in many folds.

◁ BROOCH, 13TH CENTURY.

▽ A LADY OF 1300 wearing a linen band beneath her chin. Her hair is also bound in a band of linen.

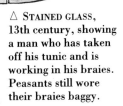

▷ THIRTEENTH-CENTURY COUPLE. The woman wears a wimple and the man a coif under a cap. Top garments with empty hanging sleeves were popular.

Men's underwear was a tuniclike shirt, and short breeches, called braies. These were the barbarian trousers, now shorter and hidden by the tunic. Long hose, like stockings made of cloth, came up to meet them. Women's underwear was just a shift. Underpants were unknown.

1066 1160 Crusader, 1265. English, 1330. Italian, 1385. Plate armor, 1450.

ARMOR AND TOURNAMENTS

PROTECTIVE CLOTHING for warfare has been in use since battles began. Chain mail and plate armor were known in the ancient world. The Greeks had plate armor of bronze, and the Romans wore hinged metal plates. Mail probably originated in the East, but was used in Europe from the second century A.D. The art of making armor from large metal plates seems to have been lost during the Dark Ages.

Eleventh-century soldiers wore a tunic made of mail, called a hauberk. It covered the upper arms and head. Soon the hauberk was given more protection. A quilted garment went under it; arm plates were strapped on. Later, a reinforced tunic was added over it. By the fourteenth century, breastplates and backplates were worn, and from these the complete suit of armor developed.

▷ KNIGHTS JOUSTING IN A TOURNAMENT. They are separated by a "tilt" or barrier, and their aim is to topple their opponent. Because it is a friendly contest, they use blunted swords and lances. Tournament armor was sometimes made of *cuir bouilli* (leather hardened by being dipped in very hot water and baked in a mold). Breastplates and backplates were often pierced with holes to make them lighter.

The crest, made of *cuir bouilli*, is held in place by an iron spike attached to the helmet.

△ THE MAIL SHIRT, or hauberk, was extended in the 12th century to cover arms and legs. The 13th-century knight wears a cylindrical helmet, a long cloth surcoat over his hauberk, and thigh protectors. The 14th-century knight's limbs are protected by metal plates. The Englishman's surcoat, short in front, may cover a breastplate. The 15th-century knight wears complete plate armor.

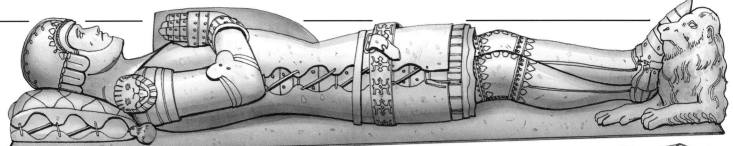

Closed helmets posed a problem as they made their wearers unrecognizable. For identification, knights wore distinctive patterns on their surcoats and crests on their helmets. This was the origin of heraldry. Fantastic crests and heraldic surcoats were worn at tournaments.

Modern experiments have shown that it is quite easy and not particularly tiring to move about in armor, though the helmet is very stuffy. In the seventeenth century, armor had to be made thick enough to resist newly invented firearms. This made it too heavy, so it was no longer used.

△ EFFIGY OF A 14TH-CENTURY KNIGHT. He is wearing a coat of plates made of overlapping bands of iron riveted to fabric. It can be seen under the lacings of his tight surcoat.

A PADDED ARMING CAP supported the helmet, which was also lined with canvas, packed with wool.

▽ TOURNAMENTS WERE MOCK BATTLES. They were dangerous competitions at first, a form of combat training, but by the late Middle Ages rules had made them safer.

▷ A SUIT OF PLATE ARMOR and its under-garments, 15th century. Cloth padding went around the knees to stop the leg armor chafing.

▷ A 15TH-CENTURY KNIGHT puts on his armor. First he gets into his shirt and braies. Then he puts on his hose and a special arming doublet, and ties up the "points" that fasten the tops of his hose to the bottom of his doublet. He no longer needs to wear a complete hauberk under his plate armor. Mail is attached to the doublet where necessary. Sleeves of mail protect his armpits and elbows.

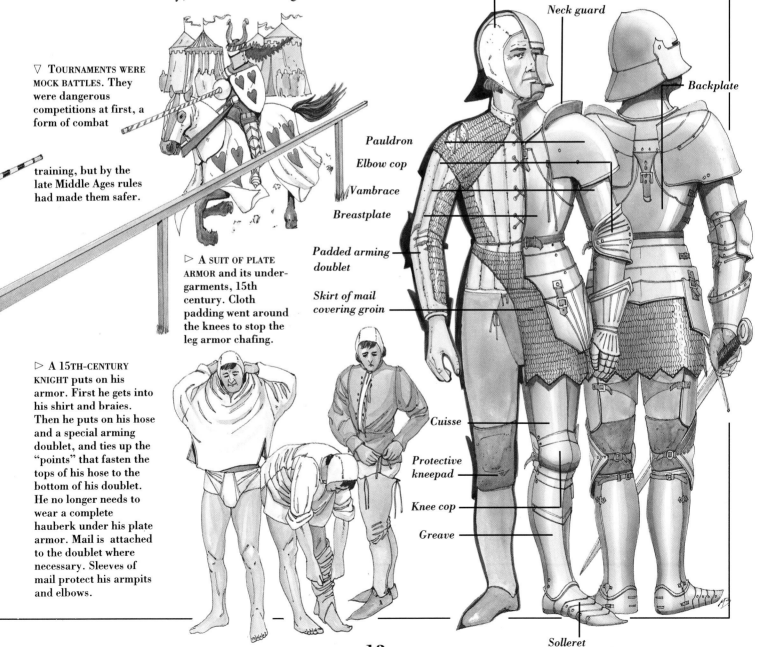

Coif

Neck guard

Backplate

Pauldron

Elbow cop

Vambrace

Breastplate

Padded arming doublet

Skirt of mail covering groin

Cuisse

Protective kneepad

Knee cop

Greave

Solleret

△ DETAIL OF A BELT.

◁ THE MAN WEARS a short, tight garment, later known as a doublet. His clothes are fashionably parti-colored and his hood ends in a long tail, called a liripipe.

△ ENGLISH NOBLES, 1350.

MEDIEVAL TIMES

THE FOURTEENTH AND FIFTEENTH CENTURIES saw the start of what can truly be called fashion. In the past the clothes of one generation had not been so different from those of the one before. Princes and nobles had worn fine clothes, and peasants rough, hardwearing ones. But now there was a new class of prosperous townspeople who wanted to compete with their rulers in display. Styles of clothes, shoes, and headgear varied as people dressed to show what extravagances they could afford. As a reaction, laws were passed stating exactly what each class of person was allowed to wear. Silks and fine furs were restricted to the nobility.

▷ PEASANTS. The woman's gown shows her chemise.

◁ MERCHANT with hood wrapped around his head fashionably, 1380.

Fourteenth-century clothes were much more body-hugging than before. Buttons began to be used for front and sleeve fastenings. Men's chests were padded to suggest manly strength, and belts were slung low on the hips.

▽ BURGUNDIANS, 1460s. Their clothes are very dandified. One man dangles an extra hat on the end of a liripipe.

▽ THE WOMAN'S GOWN reveals the lacing of her undergown. Her steeple hat was one of many fantastic styles.

◁ A TOP GARMENT called a houppelande was worn by both sexes. This one has jagged edges and is slit for riding.

▽ LONG-TOED SHOES were in fashion.

△ WOMEN IN THE 14TH CENTURY wore long-sleeved undergowns, fitted to the hips, and overgowns.

▽ BELT CHAIN. Women kept purses on a chain under their gowns, which had slits for the hands to pass through.

△ DETAIL of 15th-century velvet.

◁ YOUNG ITALIAN, 1470. Over his doublet and hose he wears an open-sided tunic. The sleeves are made in separate pieces and laced on. The shirt or chemise is puffed out through the lacings at the elbow, wrist, and shoulder.

▷ ITALIAN WOMAN, 1488, in a rich brocade overgown and an undergown and chemise (*shown above*).

During the fifteenth century, men's doublets, which already seemed shockingly short to some people, became even shorter, to just below the waist, and some young men wore them with no overgarment. The laced-up tops of women's gowns were molded to the figure with stiffening.

△ THE YOUNG MAN gets dressed. His hose are in separate legs, with a gap at the top.

△ ITALIAN CHILDREN. The todder is in underwear.

▽ A CODPIECE was a bag of material introduced to fill the gap between the hose at the front, which was revealed when a short doublet was worn.

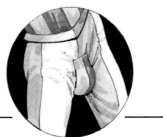

The Burgundians were the leaders of fashion in northern Europe. They favored broad shoulders and wasp-waisted doublets, and for women, extremely wide or tall headgear. Italian clothes were less bizarre, relying on rich fabrics for effect.

15

△ GERMAN COUPLE, 1514. By this time garments with slashed material were popular all over Europe.

FARTHINGALES

BY THE SIXTEENTH CENTURY, fashionable people had given up the flowing lines of medieval clothes. Rich patterned textiles, velvets and fine silks were preferred. The use of this type of fabric meant that the resulting shapes were stiff. Clothes were brightly colored. There was a craze for making slashes in clothing and pulling the material underneath through the slits.

△ SWISS AND GERMAN soldiers at the end of the 15th century started the fashion of slashing.

◁ GERMAN PEASANTS, early 16th century. One wears an old-fashioned hooded cape under his hat. The woman's headgear is medieval.

Men looked very wide and top-heavy, with broad padded shoulders, short-skirted doublets, and short top garments with large collars and puffed sleeves. Shoes were square-toed. Women's gowns had wide necklines reaching to the armpits. The skirts of overgowns were often open in front.

▽ A FRENCH FAMILY OF THE 1560s. Both parents and child wear small ruffs, a new Spanish fashion.

▽ ENGLISH NOBLEMAN, 1540, in a puff-sleeved overgown and flat cap.

▽ A TRADESMAN and a middle-class Englishwoman, 1540.

◁ 1540s ENGLISH NOBLEWOMAN. The sleeves of her magnificent silk gown are lined with fur.

The farthingale, a Spanish garment, was popular from the 1540s on. It was an underskirt inset with wicker hoops, which held out women's skirts in a cone shape. From the 1580s the French farthingale with a wide, wheel-shaped top was worn in northern Europe. This was really a court garment. Ordinary women made do by tying a sausage-shaped cushion under their skirts.

△ HIGH-SOLED SHOES for women, originally a Venetian fashion, were sometimes exaggerated.

▷ HANGING PURSES were useful, since women did not have pockets until the 19th century.

The fashions of Spain, the most powerful nation in Europe at this time, were copied everywhere in the second half of the century. The Spaniards liked dark colors, and wore padded, high-necked doublets and short cloaks. Their chins were held up by stiff shirt ruffles, which developed into wide detachable ruffs. Trunk hose, a combination of smooth-fitting knitted hose and very short breeches stuffed out with padding, were worn.

△ UNDERGARMENTS FOR WOMEN. The corset was stiffened with metal or whalebone.

△ SPANISH NOBLES of the 1570s. His fur-lined coat is worn like a cloak.

△ MENSWEAR. The pumpkin-shaped breeches were made to show the cloth beneath.

▷ JEWEL PRESENTED by Queen Elizabeth to Sir Francis Drake in 1579.

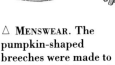

▽ MAN OF 1580. His doublet is padded so that it bulges out.

▽ RUFFS WERE SUPPORTED on wire frames. They were starched and pleated with hot metal rods.

▷ ENGLISH NOBLES, 1600. The woman wears a fan-shaped ruff and a French farthingale.

△▽ GERMAN FURRIER and hatmaker's stores.

17TH CENTURY

FASHIONS BECAME SOFTER in the first half of the seventeenth century. Farthingales went out of fashion and lace collars replaced ruffs. Styles varied from country to country. In Holland, the ruff remained in fashion and grew to the size of a cartwheel. Wealthy people tended to copy what the French were wearing. Under Louis XIV the French court was the most brilliant in Europe and gave French fashion a lead it has kept until today.

Riding clothes influenced men's styles in the first half of the century. Boots, spurs, and plumed hats were worn indoors and out. Women's clothes changed little in overall shape during the century. From the 1680s the outline became narrower and stiffer and the fullness of the skirt was swept to the back.

△ FLEMISH COUPLE, 1610. The man's wide collar is a floppy version of the fan-shaped ruff, which now falls on the shoulders.

△ THE WOMAN wears a big ruff and a long bodice that comes out over the stomach. This style was popular in the Netherlands.

◁ MEN'S CHANGING SHAPES. *Left*, 1590s' padded peasecod doublet. *Right*, ruff and breeches, 1620.

△ FASHIONABLE FRENCH CLOTHES, 1630s. Men's hair is much longer. The central woman's neckwear is midway between ruff and collar.

◁ "CAVALIER" STYLE, 1640, with high-waisted doublet, longer, tighter breeches, and boots.

△ AN IVORY FLEA TRAP, hung around the neck. A piece of blood-soaked cloth was put inside to attract fleas away from the wearer.

△ SPANISH PENDANT (*above*), 1640.

▷ COURT LADY OF 1640. The hair was flat on top and frizzed at the sides. A short rope of pearls was the favorite 17th-century necklace.

△ THE FASHIONABLE MAN had lavish accessories. Bucket-topped boots, often with lace turned down over the tops, were essential in the first half of the century. Shoes for the first time had heels. Gloves had large, decorated cuffs.

◁ FRENCH peasant family.

▽ DUTCH FAMILY, 1665. The sober-colored styles worn by certain pious Dutch families influenced the clothes of the Puritans in England and the early settlers in America.

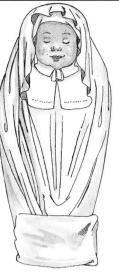

△ A BABY IN SWADDLING CLOTHES, 1665. European babies had their limbs bound tightly to their bodies.

During the 1660s men dressed more like women, in "petticoat breeches" with ribbon trims and legs so wide that they looked like skirts. People used to get the whole of themselves into one leg, by mistake. Their shirts bloused out below very brief doublets. Hair styles were so long that it was simpler to wear a wig.

△ ▷ WELL-TO-DO CHILDREN. *Above*, French. *Right*, Dutch. The boy's breeches are in the latest fashion.

▽ AMERICAN baby and mother, dressed in European fashions.

Some people disapproved of the flamboyant French fashions. Many religious Protestants, for example, felt that French fashion was too worldly. Rich merchant families in the Netherlands preferred to dress simply in black, partly from Spanish influence, but also because they believed it was more important to serve God than to wear fine clothes.

◁ RICH DUTCHMAN in stylish black. *Right*, his underwear. *Far left*, Dutch men and women in a garden, 1660s.

Charles II of England rejected exaggerated "skirts" for men, saying that he preferred "a vest in the Persian manner" with a narrow coat and simple breeches. This is thought to be the origin of the modern suit.

▽ CONTRASTS IN STYLE. Louis XIV (*left*) and Charles II in the 1670s.

▽ COAT, 1670s. Frenchman, 1680. Coats soon became fashionable.

▽ A COAT worn with no vest. Dressing gown for receiving visitors, 1690s.

▽ FRENCH ARISTOCRATS, 1694. Tall head-pieces were in fashion.

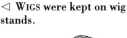
◁ WIGS were kept on wig stands.

COURT CLOTHES

THE ELABORATE CLOTHES of the French court set the fashion scene. French silks, woven in exquisite patterns, were considered to be the finest in the world, and both men's and women's styles were designed to display them. Very few people could afford such clothes, but many tried to imitate them. In the first half of the century, men's coats had wide, stiffened skirts and big cuffs. The fashion for wigs, far from dying out, went on until the 1780s. They were powdered with chalk or flour. Women did not wear wigs but powdered their own hair.

△ WORKING CLOTHES, MID-CENTURY. This French mother is not very rich and is dressed like a servant. A lady's maid would look smarter.

△ THE GIRL (*left*) wears a special cap to protect her head if she falls over. Both young boys and girls wore dresses.

▽ ENGLISH GENTLEMAN, 1755. He carries his fashionable cocked hat under his arm.

▽ COLONIAL AMERICANS in up-to-date styles. Dressed dolls were used to spread fashion news abroad before the days of fashion plates.

▽ THE WOMAN WEARS A CHEMISE, a corset, and a pannier. The man has flannel drawers. He will tie a lace cravat around his neck.

Women's skirts became much wider, with the fabric supported by side hoops made of cane. By the 1740s, some fashionable dresses were nearly 16 feet across, and women had to go through doors sideways.

▷ ENGLISHWOMAN, 1755, in a formal gown of brocaded silk. It is open in front over a long, boned bodice.

In the 1770s, women's hairstyles grew very tall. The hair was pulled up over a large stuffed pad and held in place with grease, hairpins, and powder. The pads tended to give people headaches and wire frames were later used instead. Fantastic decorations went on top, some in the form of ships, windmills and flowers. Hairdressers were so expensive that styles were left untouched for as long as possible, providing a home for fleas and lice.

△ HAIRSTYLES OF THE 1770s. Some were topped with flowers.

△ A CALECHE (*right*), a frame to protect the hair outdoors.

In the latter part of the century, simpler English clothes were admired and copied abroad. Rich Englishmen spent a lot of time on their country estates and liked to wear smarter versions of country clothes in town.

▽ 1770s CARICATURE OF A "MACARONI," an oversmart Englishman, in tight coat and tall wig.

▷ THE FATHER wears no wig and has a woolen frock coat with turned-down collar. His riding hat is the forerunner of the top hat.

▷ FRENCH ARISTOCRAT, 1777, in court dress cut away by the artist to show her underwear. Very wide skirts were now worn on formal occasions only.

Head-scratcher

▽ ENGLISH ARISTOCRATS in the country, 1770s. The mother wears a riding habit. The children, no longer dressed like adults, wear comfortable clothes. The boy is in trousers.

△ THE LADY'S COMPANION wears a powdered wig, a braided and embroidered silk suit, and white silk stockings.

△ FANS were in fashion. Detail of a painted fan of about 1730.

POLITICS

BETWEEN 1780 AND 1800, European fashions altered dramatically. Exciting new ideas of freedom and social reform were in the air. The French Revolution, which tried to replace an unjust government with one in which everyone was free and equal, put these ideas into practice in a way that changed every aspect of people's lives.

When the revolution began, people showed their support by the clothes they wore. Panniers and powdered hair, associated with the aristocrats, went out of fashion. Wealthy people chose plain dark clothes. Political extremists copied the working classes by wearing trousers instead of breeches.

△ WORKERS CELEBRATING around a "Tree of Liberty." They wear clogs, and some have only rags to put on.

△ WOMAN dressed to take part in a festival celebrating the revolution. *Right*, 1793 revolutionary. Red caps were widely worn as symbols of liberty.

△ PARISIANS OF THE 1790s. The men wear exaggerated versions of English styles.

▷ WALKING DRESSES from 1795.

▽ TRICOLOR ROSETTE in revolutionary colors, worn to prove one's loyalty.

▽ DESIGN for a citizen's costume, 1794. New men's styles were not always successful.

◁ DRESSING TO PROVOKE. After the Terror, youths in exaggerated clothes went about looking for trouble.

The extremists made France a republic in 1792, and executed the king. They started a campaign of political persecution, known as the Terror. Anyone suspected of not supporting the revolution was in danger of the death sentence. Fashion was forgotten, but clothes had never been more important. Clothes that looked too expensive, or colors such as green, which suggested royalist leanings, could lead to the wearer being accused of treachery.

▽ COUPLE OF 1800. The flimsy dresses were often dampened to make them cling to the body.

△ CARTOON, 1800, making fun of the efforts older women took to look good in the new styles.

△ FRENCH FASHIONS, 1802. The dress looks like the underwear of a few years past.

◁ THE RIDING HAT is changing into the top hat.

The men have short hair and big cravats. The man in the center wears a bicorne hat.

△ A PAD held out the skirt. Drawers were worn under very thin dresses, for decency.

▷ ENGLISH COURT DRESS, 1806. Ceremonial clothes preserved old fashions. *Right*, young Spanish noblewoman.

△ CORSETS, 1810. Many women needed some help in achieving a natural girlish shape.

When the Terror ended in 1794, the French copied the styles of ancient Greece and Rome as a way of expressing the freedom of the new republic. Women tried to look like classical statues, in thin, high-waisted white cotton dresses.

△ SKIN-TIGHT light-colored trousers were replacing knee breeches as fashionable legwear.

1 English countryman still in breeches, 1810.
2 English fashion, 1808.
3 Mother in Grecian bonnet, and boy, 1808.

4 French couple, 1814. Handbags were used when dresses grew too narrow for pockets to be hidden underneath.

5 Fashions of 1817.
6 A redingote, a long-skirted overcoat worn for riding or traveling, 1819.

Diamond head-ornament, 1800.

THE MILITARY

A UNIFORM MAKES A CLEAR STATEMENT about its wearer, a coded message that can be read at a distance, so it is not surprising that the army and navy have used it with splendid effect. Attempts at uniforms began in the seventeenth century when rulers started their own permanent armies. Before then, professional soldiers had hired themselves to fight for any ruler who paid them, and they provided their own clothes.

△ PRUSSIAN GRENADIER, 1813 (*left*). Dutch hussar, 1823 (*right*).

▽ AMERICAN SAILOR.

179th Highlanders' cap badge.

△ BRITISH GRENADIER sergeant, 1790, wearing the British soldier's traditional red coat and grenadier's fur hat.

▽ ADMIRAL NELSON'S dress uniform coat. It bears the insignia of the various Orders bestowed on him. Below is a detail of his coat button.

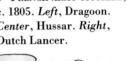

▽ FRENCH ARMY OFFICERS, c. 1805. *Left*, Dragoon. *Center*, Hussar. *Right*, Dutch Lancer.

95th Rifles' cap badge.

◁ HUSSARS (*center*) were originally Hungarian horsemen. The braided jacket derives from the Hungarian caftan, and the corded belt from a picketing rope.

▽ FRENCH *VIVANDIERES* (sellers of food and drink), 1860. They supplied refreshments to the army and wore a version of regimental uniform.

French imperial badge, 1812.

▽ 1890 BRITISH cavalry regiments. Officers of:
1 14th Hussars.
2 Royal Horse Guards.

3 10th Hussars.
4 5th Dragoon Guards.
5 5th Lancers.
6 2nd Dragoon Guards, Royal Scots Grays.

▽ SINCE WORLD WAR II, lighter and stronger fabrics have been developed for uniforms.

The success of King Frederick the Great's new Prussian army of the 1750s spurred other military leaders to copy his methods. Frederick believed in discipline and uniform. He dressed his men in short coats, and white waistcoats and breeches kept clean with chalk. They wore powdered hair in two tight curls and a pigtail. By 1800, armies in both Europe and America wore regimental uniforms in national colors. Uniforms were also introduced in the navy.

▽ U.S. ARMY UNIFORMS.
1 War of Independence.
2 War of 1812.
3 Mexican War.
4 Civil War.
5 Spanish-American War.
6 World War I.
7 World War II.
8 Korean War.
9 Vietnam War.

▽ INFANTRY UNIFORMS of World War I. *Left to right:* British, French, and German.

1 American sailor, 1940.
2 U.S. army officer, 1970.
3 British paratrooper, 1983.
4 Israeli infantrywoman.

Before 1850, armies wore bright colors, or white in hot climates, but deadlier weapons made camouflage essential. Khaki was first used in India in 1846. At first it was thought to look slovenly, but it was so practical that it became standard British wear by 1900. All forces in World War I had dull-colored uniforms. Modern combat gear appeared for airborne troops in the 1940s.

△ FASHIONS OF 1827. Women's skirts are getting fuller and their shoulders wider.

△ GERMAN mother and daughter in puffed-out sleeves, father and son in frock coats, 1833.

The girl's drawers are just tubes tied on her legs, and show beneath her skirt.

△ COUPLE of the early 1850s. Many petticoats, some of stiff horsehair, hold out the skirt.

△ AN EVENING DRESS of 1860. The skirt is held out in a circle by a crinoline.

THE CRINOLINE

THE SOBER APPEARANCE that the French Revolution had given men's clothes became the dominant fashion in the nineteenth century. Trousers, which had been worn only by working people, became normal fashionable wear, and plain dark clothes were thought to be the most suitable for men.

Women's fashions, on the other hand, grew more and more elaborate, as if to show that their husbands were so rich that they need not work. In 1857 the crinoline, a cage of flexible steel hoops that hung from the waist, was introduced. It was much lighter than petticoats had been, enabling skirts to reach a vast size. Lavish materials (over 40 yards of silk in a dress), smothered with trimmings of ribbon, bows, flounces, and flowers, were needed for a fashionable appearance.

△ PUTTING THE DRESS on over the crinoline was not easy. This drawing is based on a photograph of how it was done at a famous dressmaker's.

▽ FASHIONABLE English seaside visitors of the 1860s. The women's skirts are swept back slightly. The young man wears a new informal fashion – a high-buttoned jacket and matching trousers, forming a suit.

1 DAYWEAR, 1865. The man wears a stylish unwaisted jacket. His companion's walking dress has the 1860s' full-backed skirt.

2 Evening clothes, 1875. For men, these now had to be black. Women wore bustles under their skirts.

3 In the early 1880s, the bustle went out of fashion and women wore narrow skirts.

4 1884. Women wore fierce corsets under bustles.

5 The man wears a bowler hat.

△ POORER WORKERS, like these 1820 English country people, took little heed of expensive fashions.

The crinoline was worn by women of all classes, in spite of its inconvenience for work. In other ways, the clothes of the rich and the poor, like their lives, were very different. Women worked long hours in dressmakers' workshops, painstakingly handstitching in cramped conditions for very low wages, in order to produce the luxurious clothes worn by the rich. A rush order might mean a seamstress worked late into the night. The sewing machine, invented in the 1850s, helped to speed up the work. Some ready-made clothes appeared, but the wealthy still had each item of dress individually made for them.

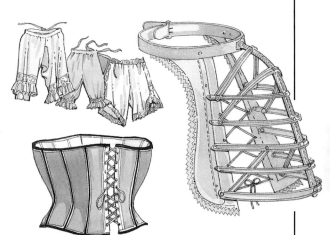

△ YOUNG GIRL'S corset, 1868, and pairs of drawers (above).

△ BUSTLE FRAMEWORK, 1887, worn with a petticoat.

FOLK COSTUME

1 Romanians.
2 Yugoslavians.
3 Hungarian couple.
4 Italians.
5 Finnish couple.
6 Polish bridal couple.
7 Greeks from Chios.
8 Russian peasants.
9 Swiss couple.

EUROPEAN NATIONAL COSTUMES are based on the clothes worn by country people. Because peasants were usually poor and traveled little, they were hardly affected by changing city fashions. As a result, their clothes preserved bygone styles. Nineteenth-century country women wore laced bodices, much as they had done in the sixteenth century.

▽ SWEDISH COUPLE (*left*), 19th century, dressed for church.

▽ NORWEGIAN COUPLE (*center*). Local styles were well preserved in Norway's villages.

▽ DENMARK. The girl's lace-trimmed bonnet shows that she is from the island of Falster.

G.WOOD

On special occasions, such as church festivals, family christenings, weddings and funerals, country people wore their best clothes, with styles of headdress and embroidery that varied from region to region and even from village to village. The materials were usually homespun. Colorful decorations, like combs, jewelry, lace, and ribbons, were bought from visiting pedlars, so that the styles of dress grew gradually more elaborate.

△ FRENCH COUPLE. The woman's red hood and plait with pompoms are typical of the Pyrenees.

The man is wearing a broad-lapelled jacket and sash. They both wear gaiters.

△ 19TH-CENTURY GERMAN COUPLE from Pomerania, wearing their Sunday clothes.

In the nineteenth century, educated people became interested in studying peasant traditions. They felt that the ways of country people represented the true character of a nation, and should be preserved. Villagers were encouraged to wear traditional dress, and societies were formed to revive it where it had died out. This gave country people fresh pride in their traditional clothes, which many had abandoned as old-fashioned. New variations appeared and trimmings became even more lavish, so that festival dress today is more splendid than ever, though in many places it is put on self-consciously for the tourists.

△ DUTCH MAN from Volendam and a woman from Marken. False curls were sometimes used on the caps.

△ A BELGIAN MILKMAID and tradesman, 19th century.

▷ THE SPANISH WOMAN (*left*) is from the Pyrenees and her companion from Salamanca.

▷ PORTUGUESE festival dress (*right*).

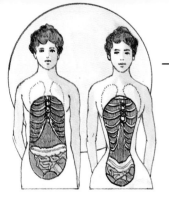

△ THE BAD EFFECTS of tight corsets, diagram of 1904.

▽ RIGID CORSET of 1883.

▽ FRENCH DRAGONFLY BROOCH, 1898, of gold, enamel, ivory, and gem stones, to be worn on an evening gown.

DRESS REFORM

DURING THE NINETEENTH CENTURY, critics often pointed out that women's fashions had become unhealthy and ridiculous. In 1851, an American, Mrs. Bloomer, tried unsuccessfully to set a better example by wearing harem-style trousers, nicknamed bloomers. Some women wore uncorseted dresses, but most people believed that tight corsets were essential, though doctors warned that they squashed the internal organs. By the 1880s, a clothes reform movement in England recommended looser styles. A German, Dr. Jaeger, also urged people to wear woolen underwear to let the skin breathe.

△ 1886 ADVERTISEMENT for "Good Sense" corsets. Even young girls wore corsets.

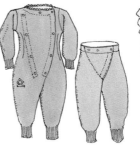

△ SOCKS WITH TOES.

◁ WOOLEN UNDERWEAR, 1886, as recommended by Dr. Jaeger.

▷ ENGLISH DRESS in Liberty silk, 1888, worn by wealthy women who thought that modern fashions were ugly.

Good advice had very little effect on fashionable clothes. From 1900 women wore a new type of corset, long and absolutely straight in front. It was supposed to be more healthy because it did not squeeze the stomach. It nipped the back extra hard instead, so it was medically not a great improvement.

▷ BOATING OUTFIT, 1902. Flannel suit, straw hat, and stiff collar with bow tie. *Below*, the wearer's pajamas, which replaced the nightshirt, and his underwear.

▷ AMERICAN LONGSHOREMEN, 1910. The majority of people did not spend their day changing from one set of leisure clothes to the next. These men, who have emigrated from Europe, would have few other clothes.

△ SILK PAJAMAS and woolen underwear.

△ UNDER HER DRESS the well-dressed woman of 1907 wore a silk camisole and a silk taffeta waist-petticoat.

Below these went one or more cotton petticoats trimmed with ribbon, and a pair of long, frilly knickers.

Under that: a cotton chemise under a long corset, which pushed the front of the body up and bent it behind.

Hobble garter, 1910.

Hobble skirt, 1913.

△ THEATER COSTUME, 1911, by Leon Bakst, who designed for the Russian ballet.

△ WEALTHY COUPLE AT THE RACES, 1903. The man wears formal morning dress, still seen today at weddings.

His companion's dress has ruffles cascading over the bust. The new corsets shaped busts into a sloping surface.

▽ WOMEN WAR WORKERS. *Left*, farm worker. *Center*, factory worker. *Right*, factory superintendent.

▷ A YOUNG WOMAN OF 1919. Her clothes suggest that she wants to look capable and independent.

Wealthy people had special types of clothing for each social occasion and might change their clothes six times a day. The visit of the Russian ballet to Paris in 1910 made oriental styles all the rage. Suddenly rigid bodices were out of fashion. Softer dresses, turbans, and feather plumes were worn. At the same time skirts became so narrow that women had to join their legs with "hobble garters" to stop them taking steps long enough to split the seams. The 1914-18 war put a stop to such exaggerated fashions. Many women were doing the jobs of men away fighting, and needed sensible clothes.

SPORTSWEAR

UNTIL THE NINETEENTH CENTURY, people did not wear special clothes for sports. Men just took off their coats to play. Women on the whole did not take part. From the 1820s it was usual to wear certain clothes for certain sports, although they had not been specially designed for the purpose. Cricketers, for instance, usually wore white trousers and shirts. They also played in top hats, because gentlemen at that time were not correctly dressed without them. The earliest football clothes, which appeared in the 1860s, were jerseys, knickerbockers, pill-box caps, and boots. In the 1880s, knee-length football shorts came in.

Foam collar

Facemask

Cross-section of helmet

Shoulder pads

Arm pads

Rib pads

▷ FOOTBALL PLAYERS need shock-absorbent helmets and protective padding for shoulders, ribs, and thighs.

Hip pads

Thigh pads

△ EARLY HELMETS were based on leather flying helmets. Plastic was first used in 1939. Today's helmet (cut away) is reinforced.

◁ MODERN SOCCER PLAYER (left) and 1920s' player.

▽ WEIGHT LIFTERS are helped by light clothing.

Shin pads

Ankle tape

▷ TODAY'S FOOTBALL PLAYER and a player of 1907 (behind).

▽ AN ICE HOCKEY GOALKEEPER wears helmet, mask, throat protector, body pad, and arm, knee, shoulder and goal pads.

Women took up sports later in the nineteenth century. But people believed so firmly that short skirts were indecent and thin clothing unhealthy, that it was some time before sports clothes for women appeared. In the 1880s, bolder women wore short dresses over bloomers, with stockings, gaiters, and boots. By the 1890s, a simpler style, with long skirt, blouse, and boater hat, was worn by women for outdoor activities and sports.

▷ 18TH-CENTURY BOXERS. The modern boxing star (*right*) promotes a brand.

Sports influence the way all of us dress, for the sportswear of one era becomes the everyday dress of the next. Culottes, for example, invented for cycling, were accepted in the 1930s as leisure wear and are now frequently worn by businesswomen. Today, the process has speeded up. Sweatshirts, tracksuits, and Lycra shorts, which most people wear as casual clothes, all began as sportswear.

△ LAWN TENNIS, 1881. In a narrow dress in latest French fashion, this woman will not be playing a fast game.

△ SUZANNE LENGLEN (*left*) pioneered the short tennis dress in the 1920s. Today, men and women dress alike.

▽ THIS CYCLIST wears gear made with Lycra, a stretch fiber invented in the 1970s.

▽ BATHERS SHED their clothes over the years. Bathing costumes of 1871, 1920, and today.

△ GOLF IN BUSTLES, 1873, and (*center*) in 1890s knickerbocker suits and serge skirts.

In the 1920s (*right*), women wore divided skirts, while men wore baggy knickerbockers.

▽ WOMEN CYCLISTS of the 1890s were laughed at for wearing loose knickerbockers.

▽ CRICKET CLOTHES. Schoolboys,1771 (*left*). Cricketer, 1847 (*top right*). Modern player (*below*). Protective clothing was not worn until the late 1800s.

BETWEEN THE WARS

D URING THE 1920s AND 1930s, simple, comfortable clothes became fashionable, especially for women. In past times, the rich buyers of fashion had plenty of leisure to visit the dressmaker. Now, society had changed. Women who might previously have automatically gone into domestic service now had a choice, and many preferred to work in factories and offices. They needed simple, sensible work clothes. Wealthier people found it more difficult to find servants and had to do more for themselves, such as laundering and caring for their clothes and running a household. They no longer wanted fashions that needed a lot of care.

△ FRENCH FASHION PLATE, 1923, showing elegant afternoon dresses with low waists.

The fashionable shape was flat-chested. Busty women wore chest-flattening bras.

▷ A TRAVELING TOILET CASE, with equipment for beauty care.

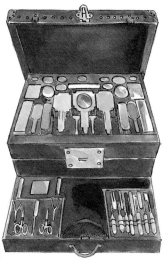

◁ TRAVELING WOMEN, 1924. Their trunks have special pull-out boxes for shoes.

△ THIS WELL-DRESSED woman of 1924 wears a two-piece, pleated woolen dress.

△ THE MAN'S LOUNGE SUIT, bowler hat, and turned-down collar are right for town.

▷ 1926 SUIT by the designer Chanel, who made simple dressing fashionable.

◁ PENDANT with case for lipstick, which was again in use.

The easy-fitting women's clothes of the early 1920s were followed by a very boyish look, with short hair cut like men's, short skirts and flat chests produced by breast-flattening bras. Some women dressed in copies of men's suits. Skirts shot up and by 1926 were just above the knee, which many people found very shocking.

△ THE PRINCE OF WALES wears an informal peaked cap and hand-knitted Fair Isle jersey, 1925.

△ SMART CHILDREN of fashion-conscious parents, 1927, in cloche hats and high hemlines, like their mothers.

Fashion in the 1930s favored a long, sleek look, achieved with bias-cut fabrics which hugged the hips and flared at the hem. Hollywood stars were a major new fashion influence. The sunbathing cult encouraged revealing swimwear and sportswear. Sundresses were bare-backed. Both men and women wore cycling shorts.

△ BRASSIERES WERE NOW WORN. Bra of 1924 (*top*). Bra of 1929 (*bottom*).

◁ BEACHWEAR, 1929. Sunbathing was "in." Previously, wealthy people had avoided the sun because tanned skin was associated with being a worker.

△ PERMANENTLY WAVED HAIR, 1933. Hollywood film stars popularized bleached hair.

In the past, garments had been handmade to order to fit individual customers. Poor people could not afford to pay for the work that went into fashion clothes. In the twenties and thirties this changed. Despite much unemployment, those who had work tended to have better pay than in the past. Magazines, advertising, and the movies told them about fashion. Clothing manufacturers began to mass-produce cheap fashion wear.

△ FORMAL DAY DRESSES, 1930. Hats are romantic, and hip-clinging skirts swirl around the calves.

◁ PEOPLE OF a British mining community, 1935. In front, a middle class child, 1933.

▽ DRESSES AND COATS with padded shoulders, 1939, for smart day wear in town.

△ SILK LOUNGING PAJAMAS for leisure and party wear, 1930.

▷ OVERCOATS, 1934. Men still usually wore hats.

Y-fronts, introduced 1934.

THE WAR AND AFTER

THE WAR YEARS were a time of shortages in many countries, as overseas trade was interrupted and factories switched to making war supplies. Fabric was used sparingly in garments, skirts grew shorter, and jerseys were unraveled and reknitted. In place of hats, women wore headscarves, and faked silk stockings by painting their legs brown, with lines on the back to imitate seams.

△ ENGLISH WOOLEN DRESS, 1941. Wartime clothes were rationed with coupons in Britain.

△ THIS 1946 PARIS GOWN would be sold to Americans, since Europeans had little money after the war.

△ THE NEW LOOK'S padded hips and long full skirts were very feminine compared with wartime styles, which were designed to save cloth.

1 Wool suit, early 50s.
2 Linen dress in the 1955 "A line" style.
3 1955 ball gown.

▷ COUPLE OF 1958, the man in a contrasting waistcoat, the woman in an A-line dress.

The French designer Christian Dior created a sensation with his 1947 "New Look" fashions. Critics called the Look ridiculous, but most women, fashion-starved by the war, tried at all costs to buy or create a form of it. For much of the fifties, long, tight-waisted styles remained in fashion.

△ CLOTHES worn by 1950s' "Beatniks" showed rejection of their elders' values.

▽ BRASSIERE, 1958, designed to give "uplift." In the 1950s, large busts were fashionable.

36

1 Tweed suit, 1962.
2 Underwear, 1966.
3 Pantie girdle, 1965.
4 Designer blazer, 1965.

From the late 1950s to the 1970s, earnings rose in developed countries. High employment produced two-income families and installment-plan buying began. This created a huge new buying public, and for the first time fashions were created specially for teenagers. Constant fashion changes, heavily advertised, kept people eager to go on buying.

Clothes became more informal. Men wore casual jackets and only wore ties on formal occasions. Women enjoyed the freedom of trousers. Young people no longer bothered with fashion rules, like matching accessories or wearing hats and gloves. They had their own world of music, and choice of music governed choice of clothes.

△ MINISKIRT, 1965. This design is by Mary Quant, whose clothes sold worldwide.

◁ THE HIPPY MOVEMENT started in the 1960s. Many young people copied its style.

△ LONDON STYLES OF 1973. Trousers were flared.

◁ HOT PANTS, an alternative to the mini-skirt, appeared in 1971.

△ FASHIONS OF THE LATE 1960S. Catsuit (*left*) and maxi-dress.

◁ WOMEN'S PANTSUITS became high fashion in the 1960s. This 1965 version has a coat instead of a jacket.

The sixties miniskirt, unlike today's version, was not an optional style worn mainly by the young. For several years, women of all ages, shapes, and sizes wore it.

△ KNICKERBOCKER SUIT (*right*) designed by Jeff Banks and layered look (*left*), from 1978.

Platform shoe, 1972.

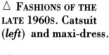

TRADITIONAL DRESS

◁ AN ELABORATELY DECORATED man's gown made by the Manding people of West Africa, who live in an area from Senegal to Ghana.

▽ AN INDIAN TURBAN ORNAMENT, of rubies and diamonds set in gold. *Below left*, 19th-century Indian prince.

NOWADAYS, WESTERN DRESS in one form or another is seen in almost every part of the world. We choose our clothes according to the way we think about ourselves. Each country has its own traditions of dress, and the kind of clothes worn internationally for business and in political life may not seem appropriate in other parts of people's lives. Even in Europe different traditions are alive, from the Scottish kilt to the peasant clothes of eastern European countries.

▽ NORTH AFRICAN WOMAN wearing a hand-printed cotton tunic dress.

1 Bedouin woman in traditional jewelry.
2 Man from Afghanistan in loose gown and trousers.
3 Modern Egyptian in traditional gallibiya.
4 Saudi Arabian in protective robe and head covering.

▽ INDIAN CLOTHES. Hindu priest in a cotton robe (*left*). Professional man in long coat and trousers (*center*). Woman in a silk sari (*right*). A sari is made of over 8 yards of material.

In many parts of Africa, the response to heat has been to wear lightweight clothes. Arabs wear all-enveloping garments to cope with sandstorms, heat and cold.

▽ PALESTINIAN embroidered linen dress from the Jaffa area.

△ ESKIMOS DRESSED in seal and caribou skins. The man's wooden hat protects his eyes.

◁ THE CHILD wears a kimono and obi. Her obi is tied in a butterfly bow. Married women tie theirs in a flat knot.

▷ JAPANESE COMBS AND HAIRPINS, worn instead of jewelry.

Japanese child.

The earliest form of Indian dress was draped. The dhoti, a loincloth tucked between the legs, and the sari belong to this tradition. Later the Indians also adopted trousers and coats from the nomads of central Asia, who wore fitted clothes that were suited to their life on horseback. The Chinese jacket or tunic worn over trousers shows the same influence. Elaborate ceremonial dress was worn at the courts of China and Japan.

▽ SCOTTISH SILVER BROOCH, with incised decoration, 18th century. These large brooches were used to fasten the plaid on the left shoulder.

◁ SCOTTISH SKEAN DHU, worn in top of sock.

◁ NORTH AMERICAN PLAINS INDIAN in deerskin shirt and trousers. The shirt is decorated with cut fringe, porcupine quills, and glass beads.

△ EARLY 20TH CENTURY Chinese dolls showing an ordinary family dressed in working clothes. They are wearing closed jackets and long tunics.

▷ SCOTSMAN in full Highland dress. The Highlanders originally wore a very long piece of plaid cloth around the waist and over the shoulder. The kilt, a version that went around the waist only, was devised early in the 18th century.

The Eskimo and Indian traditions of North America make use of animal skins, with variations in cut and decoration according to tribe. In South America, the ancient traditions of the Aztecs and Incas survive in garments like the poncho.

Sporran

WORK CLOTHES

CLOTHES CAN OFTEN TELL US WHAT A PERSON DOES, either for just a short time, like being a wedding guest or a hiker, or more permanently in his or her daily work. We would not mistake a police officer for a nurse, or a fire fighter for a butcher. Even where there is no uniform, most jobs carry an expected way of dressing. Bank managers would upset people if they arrived for work in T-shirts and sweatpants.

△ DUTCH RAT CATCHER, 18th century, vital to the warehouses of the Dutch grain trade.

▷ 1890s COWBOY. The wide-brimmed hat (*left*) kept off the sun. The neck cloth was pulled over his face in a dust storm. Leg coverings protected him from cactus growth, and gloves prevented rope burns on the hands.

▽ MASK, 17th century, worn by doctors attending plague victims.

△ GERMAN MILKMAID, 18th century.

▽ LAUNDRESS, 18th century.

◁ GERMAN MINER, 17th century. The back apron of his garment shields his legs as he pulls his wagon.

The clothes worn for some jobs have hardly changed over the centuries. These are usually professions in which dignity and tradition are important, like the Church.

Until fairly recently, working people could afford few clothes. Those they worked in might well be the only clothes they had, so wearing an apron was essential. Aprons were probably the earliest garments to be put on especially for doing work and were used in numerous jobs for keeping clean, holding tools, and gathering and carrying things. Servants' livery, countrymen's smocks, and seamen's trousers are early forms of work dress that differed from normal clothes.

▽ SCOTTISH FISHWIFE (*left*) and hospital nurse (*right*), 19th century.

▽ FEMALE STREETCAR CONDUCTOR in novel workgear.

1 Bishop. Church vestments are derived from late Roman dress.
2 Lord Chancellor.
3 Butler in tailcoat.
4 1930s movie usher.
5 Hotel bellhop.
6 Butchers' blue aprons go back to the 17th century.

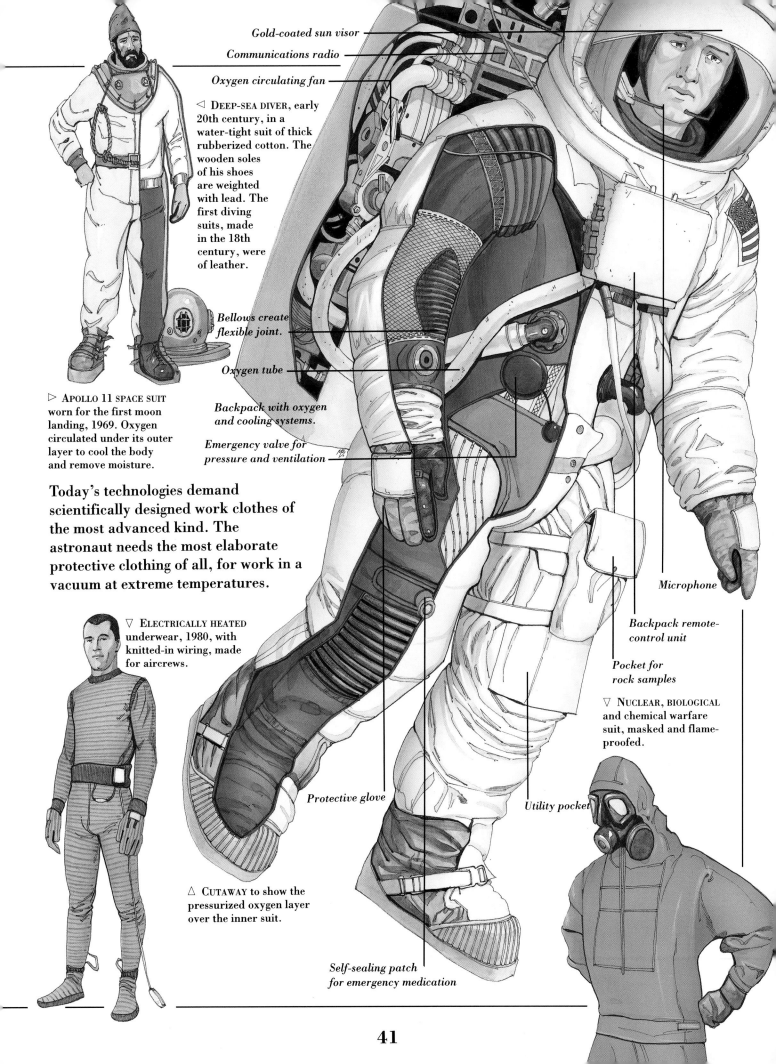

Gold-coated sun visor

Communications radio

Oxygen circulating fan

◁ DEEP-SEA DIVER, early
20th century, in a
water-tight suit of thick
rubberized cotton. The
wooden soles
of his shoes
are weighted
with lead. The
first diving
suits, made
in the 18th
century, were
of leather.

Bellows create
flexible joint.

Oxygen tube

Backpack with oxygen
and cooling systems.

Emergency valve for
pressure and ventilation

▷ APOLLO 11 SPACE SUIT
worn for the first moon
landing, 1969. Oxygen
circulated under its outer
layer to cool the body
and remove moisture.

Today's technologies demand
scientifically designed work clothes of
the most advanced kind. The
astronaut needs the most elaborate
protective clothing of all, for work in a
vacuum at extreme temperatures.

▽ ELECTRICALLY HEATED
underwear, 1980, with
knitted-in wiring, made
for aircrews.

Microphone

Backpack remote-
control unit

Pocket for
rock samples

▽ NUCLEAR, BIOLOGICAL
and chemical warfare
suit, masked and flame-
proofed.

Protective glove

Utility pocket

△ CUTAWAY to show the
pressurized oxygen layer
over the inner suit.

Self-sealing patch
for emergency medication

41

CLOTHES TODAY

MANY CHANGES have happened recently in fashion. Fashion was once created only for the rich and powerful, who chose clothes to suit them. The young had no independence and had to wear what their elders chose. In the sixties this changed dramatically when teenage earnings rose. Teenagers became the major buyers and dictated the fashions for everybody. Perhaps we have seen a reverse of this trend recently. In the 1980s and 1990s, fewer young people have jobs, and shops catering for older career women have appeared.

△ "POWER DRESSING" in the mid-1980s. Business people wanted to look very successful.

Career women aimed to look smart and not too feminine. Frilly clothes would have suggested that they needed to use their looks to succeed in their jobs. A suit was the answer.

The fitness cult brought onto the eighties fashion scene clothes that originated in the gym. Lycra shorts, originally for cycling, and stretch-fabric mini-dresses show the vogue for clothes that cling.

◁ PUNKS are now so much a part of British life that they appear on tourist postcards.

△ THE PRINCESS OF WALES became a fashion trendsetter in the 1980s. Media stars and public figures have reached similar status.

△ BRAND NAME CLOTHES played a big part in the 1980s. Without labels, cheap and expensive clothes looked alike.

◁ LEVIS. SINCE THE MID-1950s, denim jeans have been the universal casual wear for men, women, and children.

▽ SMART COUNTRY CLOTHES turn up in town just as in the 18th century. This couple in green Wellingtons and waxed jackets are walking the dog on Main Street.

△ CLOTHES for a royal race meeting, 1990. Dress preserves past traditions.

◁ LEVIS were the first jeans to be made with copper rivets.

THE FUTURE

CLOTHES THAT CHANGE COLOR with body heat are being sold today. Clothes that "think" may soon be with us, altering hue with our mood, adapting to the weather and checking radiation levels. What might they look like? In the past, today's casual wear became tomorrow's business clothes, which means that, in future, politicians may well address the United Nations wearing bodystockings.

Technology may dictate fashion in order for clothes to protect us from the polluted environment. If we use up too much of the earth's energy, everybody may have to make clothes last a lifetime. One thing is certain – we shall always wear clothes, which are the most direct means of showing status, wealth, power, occupation, allure, and awareness of fashion.

Solar disks to absorb energy and filter radiation

Antipollution oxygen mask

Control panel for temperature of suit

Decorative kneepads

Extended sneakers

△ IN A "GLOBAL VILLAGE" of the future, where world resources are conserved and shared, traditional clothes have mingled in new styles. The flat hat is a reminder of the radiation shield of the 21st century.

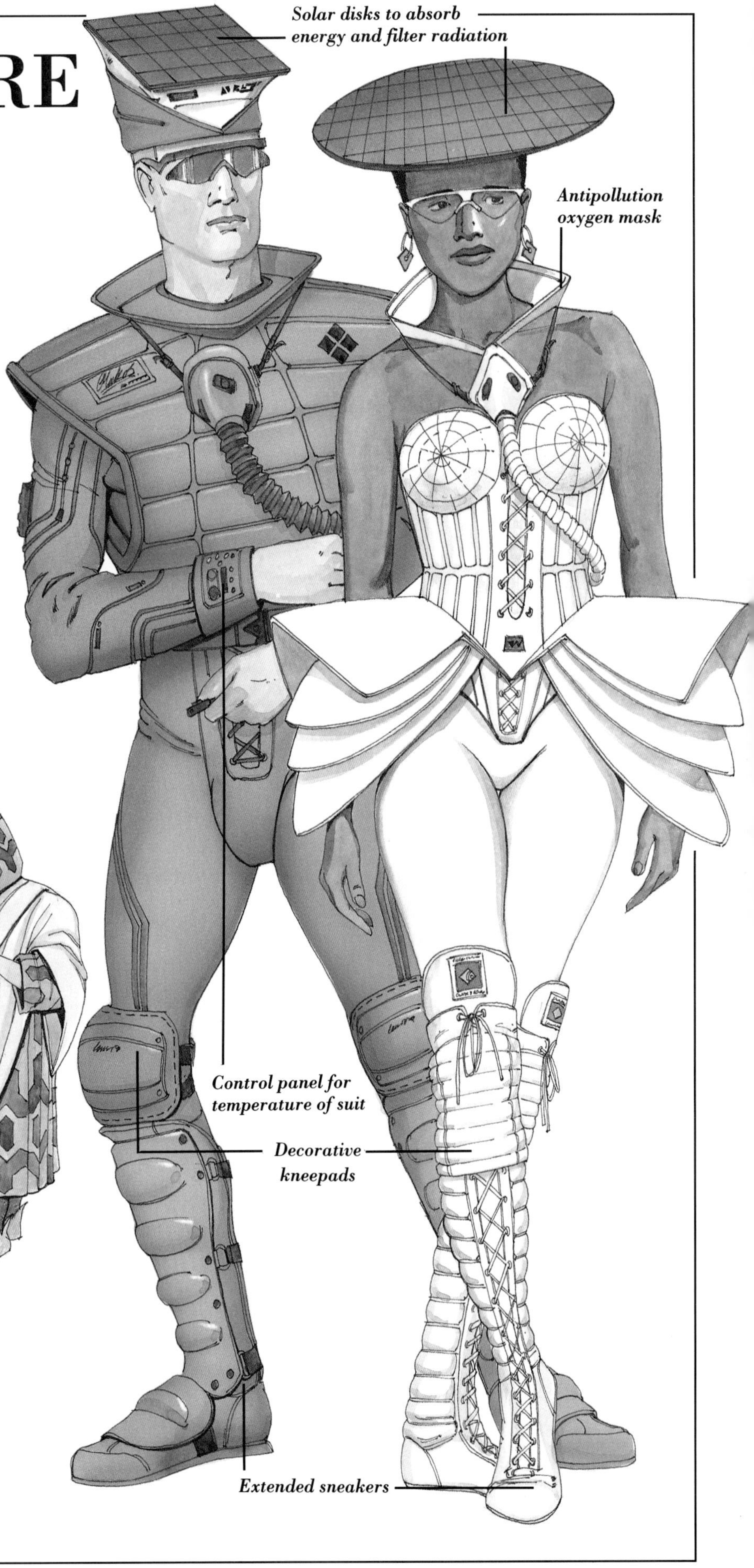

▷ TECHNOLOGY gives maximum protection in these leisure clothes of the future, which continue to show a debt to the past, like the man's laced codpiece, and the woman's corset, panniers, and 1950s bra.

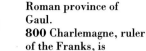

Neolithic necklace

TIMELINE

Medieval couple

B.C.
c.30,000 Bone sewing needles in use.
c.21,000 Remains of shell-decorated skin garments of this date have been found at Sungir, Russia.
c.5000 Date of oldest surviving scrap of woven cloth, which is made of linen.
c.3000 Sumerian and Egyptian civilizations in existence.
c.2600 Silk produced in China.
c.2000-1400 Minoan culture develops.
745-612 Assyrians build up and lose a great empire. Wall reliefs at Ninevah show fringed robes and curled beards.
c.700 Chiton worn in Greece.

Etruscans, 5th century

539 Persian conquerors bring trousers to the Near East.
c.500 Etruscan clothes begin to show Greek influence.
150 Romans fighting northern Teutons do not admire their roughly made trousers.
A.D.
c.100 Toga becomes smaller.
c.200 Ankle length tunic replaces the toga, which shrinks to a stole.
395 Byzantium becomes capital of the eastern half of the Roman Empire.
481 The Franks, wearing braies and tunics, take over the Roman province of Gaul.

800 Charlemagne, ruler of the Franks, is crowned emperor in Rome. He is later buried in a dalmatic edged with gold, and many layers of robes. On his feet were scarlet shoes set with emeralds. These were ceremonial clothes. He usually wore a tunic, braies, and a cloak, fur-lined for winter.
1060 The Normans capture Sicily from the Arabs and discover the luxury of Arab clothes and craftsmanship.
1066 English spies at the Battle of Hastings report that the Normans have hair so short that the backs of their necks are shaven, like a priest's.

Viking woman

1100 The Crusades reopen trade with the Near East. Rich silks and new ways of cutting clothes are introduced to the West.
c.1130 European clothes begin to be more shaped to the body.
c.1300 The man's tunic pulled over the head is gradually replaced by one that is front opening. This becomes the doublet.

c.1340-1420 Multi-colored clothes are popular.
c.1350 Veils and wimples are becoming old-fashioned. Nuns and widows still wear them.

Peasant and stained glass, 13th century

Men begin to wear their hoods tied turbanlike around their heads.
1360-1480 Men's shoes are pointed, sometimes so much so that the tips have to be stuffed.
1380-1450 A very full overgown, the houppelande, worn by both sexes.
c.1450 The hennin, a steeple-shaped headdress, is one of the century's fantastic female headgears. In France it is so tall that doorways have to be altered for it. Men's doublets become so short that a codpiece must be added to the hose.
c.1500 Slashing (pulling the lining through slits in the outer material) now in fashion, especially for men. Very broad-toed shoes are worn.
c.1530 The farthingale is brought to the French court by Eleanor of Castile, Queen of France.
c.1550 Dark Spanish fashions copied by the

Fashionable man of 1580

Byzantine rider

upper classes all over Europe.
c.1561 Queen Elizabeth of England is presented with her first pair of knitted silk hose.
c.1570 The shirt's neck frill becomes the ruff. Doublets and trunk hose are padded with "bombast" (rags, horsehair, or bran).
c.1570-1600 Varieties of legwear for men include trunk hose, "canions" (tight thigh-coverings worn under trunk hose), and "slops" (very baggy knee breeches).
1589 The Reverend William Lee invents a loom for machine-knitted stockings.
c.1610 Lace collars begin to replace ruffs.
c.1620 Men wear feathered hats and riding boots indoors and out.
1650-1700 Patches –

German peasants, 16th century

small shapes cut from black silk – are stuck on the face by men and women of fashion.
1652-70 Petticoat breeches worn by men.
1650 Men begin to wear wigs arranged in elaborate curls.
1660 A new style of dress for men appears in both England and France – a knee-length vest and coat. Together

with breeches it formed a three-piece suit, which changed little for the next century.
1680 Men wear full-bottomed wigs with masses of curls on the shoulders.
1690 It is said that a lady of Louis XIV's court tied her hair up with a garter while out hunting. The king admires the effect and an instant fashion for ribbon top-knots begins. These develop into wired lace headdresses but are out of fashion by 1699.
1700 Fashionable people begin to powder their hair. Many styles of wig appear from now on. The "campaign" wig, with curls knotted up in bunches, is worn for active pursuits. The short "bob" wig with a roll at the back of the neck is for informal wear. The "bag" wig encloses the hair in a silk pouch.
1750 Very wide hooped skirts go out of fashion, except for court dress. In

Colonial Americans

England, Jonas Hanway attracts ridicule by using an umbrella to keep off rain. Previously such things have been used, usually by women, to keep off the sun.
1760 Simpler English styles, including the coat cut away for riding, become

Women walking, 1795

fashionable for men. Men return to wearing their own hair, often still powdered.

1770 The first fashion plates are published. Women wear towering hairstyles.

1780 Queen Marie Antoinette of France wears simple chemise gowns. For the first time, children have clothes designed for them instead of being

American sailor

put in adult styles.

1792 The French Revolution. Aristocratic fashions are shunned in France. Revolutionary supporters, like workers, wear trousers. After the Terror, women ball guests wear thin red ribbons around their throats as a guillotine joke.

1800 Classical styles become popular. Women wear narrow, high-waisted dresses. Pale, skin-tight pantaloons may have been men's attempt to look like naked classical statues.

c.1810 Trousers become acceptable.

c.1816 The frock coat, with all-around skirt, appears for men.

1820 Fashionable men are tightly corseted,

and wear high, upright shirt collars almost cutting their cheeks.

1823 Scottish chemist Charles MacIntosh combines rubber and cloth and makes the first "mac."

1830 Frenchman Barthélemy Thimmonier invents the first sewing machine, which makes a single thread stitch.

1846 American Elias Howe patents a lock-stitch sewing machine. Isaac Singer markets and exports a similar machine. Charles Worth, an Englishman who becomes the most famous dressmaker in Paris, uses live models to show his new designs, which he protects by copyright. This is the start of the organized selling of very expensive designer fashion known as *haute couture*. Designers of such fashions are called *couturiers*.

1850 The turn-down shirt collar appears. Ties begin to replace

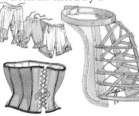

German family, 1833

cravats. Levi Strauss goes west to sell tent canvas to American miners and makes trousers from spare cloth. Later they are made from cotton twill from Nîmes, France, called *serge de Nîmes*. This is how denim got its name.

1856 The cage crinoline patented in Paris.

1860 The bowler hat appears, said to have been invented by a

European national costumes

hatter named Bowler for a client who wanted a hard hat for riding.

1865-75 The bustle is in fashion.

1878 Dr. Jaeger of Stuttgart, Germany, publishes his theories on the health benefits of woolen underwear.

1880 Men wear dinner jackets in place of tail coats for evening wear, but not until 1918 if women are present.

Scotsman in Highland dress

1881 The Rational Dress Society founded in London to campaign for more sensible clothes.

1882 The bustle makes a comeback until 1885.

1890 Trouser press invented. It produces sharp creases in trousers.

1892 A "clasp locker" patented in Chicago to replace laces for fastening boots. This is the first zipper. It is not used on clothes until the late 1920s.

1914 Backless brassiere patented by Mary Phellps Jacob. German fighter pilots cut the tails of their leather coats for convenience, producing the "bomber jacket." British forces use Thomas Burberry's

Underclothes of the 1880s

waterproof cotton coats. He gives them "trench" details of storm flaps, epaulets, and metal rings used to hold grenades.

1922 The Prince of Wales has his trousers made with turn-ups, and sets a new fashion.

1924 Rayon, an artificial fiber made from wood pulp, provides a cheap substitute for silk.

1925 Hemlines rise above the knee. But the state of Utah introduces a fine or imprisonment for women wearing skirts more than 3 inches above the ankle.

1932 Stretch girdles of Lastex replace corsets for younger women. They become known as "roll ons."

1934 Men's jockey briefs appear in the United States.

1939 "Miracle yarn" nylon displayed at 1939 World Fair.

1941-49 Clothes rationed in Britain with an average of 66 coupons a year. Eight coupons buy a pair of pajamas or a shirt in 1942.

1946 Bikini bathing suit appears.

Power dressing, 1980s

1947 Christian Dior's fashion house shows its New Look.

1954-5 The T-shirt, originally a U.S. Navy undervest, is popularized by actors Marlon Brando and James Dean in Hollywood films.

1965-68 Miniskirt hemline rises to the upper thigh. Women's knee-high boots appear.

Clothes of the future

1969 The maxi coat falls to the ankle.

1970 Ethnic clothes, flared jeans, and the romantic Laura Ashley look become popular.

1976 Punk street fashion appears.

1980 Businessmen and women begin "power dressing." Body-hugging clothes, such as leggings and cycling shorts made with Lycra, a stretchy material, become popular.

1984 The Nike "Air Jordan" trainer is launched and adopted as fashionable streetwear.

1985 The department store Bloomingdales launches its "Dynasty" collection of clothes, based on the popular TV soap opera. The Dynasty collection attracts 20,000 extra shoppers to the store.

1990 Pop singer Madonna popularizes the bustier and other undergarments designed by Jean Paul Gaultier to be worn as outerwear.

GLOSSARY

Barter To trade by exchanging goods of equal value.

Bias cut A way of cutting cloth so that the threads of the weave will hang diagonally when the garment is worn, not down and across in the usual way.

Bicorne hat Hat with the brim turned flat against the crown on both sides.

Braies Loose trousers worn by northern peoples, sometimes tied at the ankles, sometimes bound to the leg with strips of material.

Brocade A rich, stiff silk material with a woven pattern.

Bustle Padding or frame to hold out the skirt, just below the back waist.

Camisole Woman's underbodice worn from the 1840s to cover the corset.

Chemise A man's undershirt, or a woman's long undergarment, of white linen, wool, or cotton. A chemise gown is a simple, low-necked gown of thin material, resembling a chemise.

Cocked hat Hat with the brim turned up to make a three-cornered shape.

Codpiece A flap of material that covered the gap at the top of men's hose, revealed when doublets became very short, in the 15th century. In the 16th century, it was emphasized by padding. It sometimes served as a pocket.

Combinations All-in-one buttoned undergarment with long sleeves and legs, of 19th-century origin.

Cravat Men's white neckscarf.

Culottes Divided skirt.

Doublet A man's short, front-opening overgarment, sometimes padded, worn from the 14th century onwards.

Drawers An early name for knickers.

Frock coat A man's coat with a skirt of equal length all the way around.

Gaiters Leg protectors of tough cloth or leather, reaching from below the knee to the upper part of the foot.

Gallibiya North African version of a loose, all-enveloping garment worn in varying forms in Turkey, the Middle East and India.

Hobble skirt A very narrow skirt, tapering towards the ankle.

Hose Leg coverings made of wool or linen cloth, or knitted fabric. Eleventh-century hose were knee-length. Some had feet, sometimes with thin leather soles for indoor use; some ended at the ankle and might have a strap under the instep to hold them down. By the 12th century, hose were thigh-length. In the 15th century, the hose were joined at the top to form one garment, similar to modern tights.

Kimono A traditional Japanese loose overgarment with wide hanging sleeves.

Knickerbockers Loose breeches fastened below the knee.

Leg warmers Knitwear tubes worn in concertina folds on the lower leg.

Liripipe The long, taillike end of a hood, which developed in the 14th century as decorative exaggeration of the hood's tip.

Lounge suit Daytime suit of matching jacket, trousers, and waistcoat, worn from the 1870s. It was then the most casual way to dress. Today's version is formal business wear.

Mail Armor made of rows of interlocked metal rings.

Mob cap A woman's round white cap with a frilled border, worn indoors in the 18th century.

Morning dress Men's daytime wear for formal occasions, worn from the late 19th century. It consisted of top hat, morning coat (a coat cut away in a curve over the hips), and trousers. It is worn today at weddings and on occasions when royalty is present.

Neolithic Belonging to a stage in humankind's development before people had discovered how to make metal. They still used stone tools, but no longer relied on hunting. They grew crops and raised animals for food. A few remote peoples have Neolithic cultures today, but in the history of civilization, Neolithic culture began around 8000 B.C.

Paleolithic The earliest phase of humankind's development, from two million years ago until around 50,000 years ago.

Panniers Supports for the wide skirts worn in the 18th century.

Pantaloons Tight-fitting, pale-colored trousers, buttoned at the ankle, popular from 1800-1850. Also a name for women's drawers.

Parti-colored Made in two materials of different colors.

Plate armor Armor made of large metal pieces, shaped to fit the body and jointed to move with the wearer.

Points Laces with metal ends.

Poncho South American cape made of a rectangle of cloth, with a central slit for the head to pass through.

Pumps Soft, flat-heeled shoes with thin soles.

Ruff A collar of stiffened ruffles, often completely encircling the neck.

Skean dhu Small knife worn by the Scots in the top of the sock.

Surcoat An overtunic, sometimes sleeveless.

Tippets Long, decorative strips of material hanging from the ends of sleeves, 13th and 14th century.

Tricorne hat A hat with brim turned back to form three points.

Undress uniform Military uniform for daily use, a less elaborate version of the full dress uniform worn on ceremonial occasions.

Vest A man's narrow, close-fitting garment, originally reaching to below the knee, worn beneath a coat.

Wimple A piece of fine white linen or silk, covering the front neck and sometimes coming up over the chin. Worn by women in the 13th and 14th centuries.

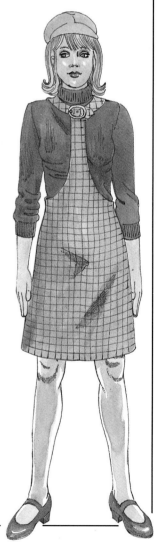

INDEX

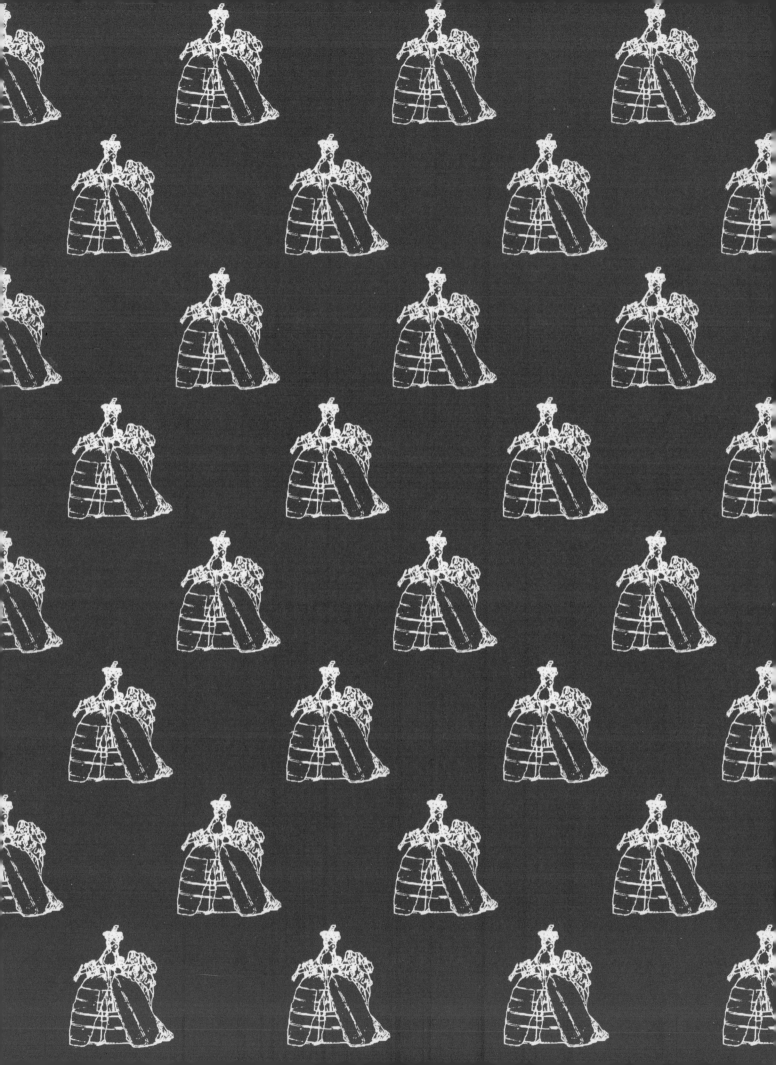